Alison Hodge

things reconstructed

featuring the work of

DAVID KEMP

contents

raw

material

raw material

"I make things out of things, big things, little things, old things and new things. I like to recycle things, and find new uses for things that have been thrown away. Some things say something about their surroundings, and other things become something else."

David Kemp. January 2002

raw material

raw
material

material

place of work

For more than 20 years, David Kemp has lived and worked on the exposed Atlantic coast of west Cornwall – inspired by the natural landscape, and by the remains of the tin-mining industry carried out there since medieval times. Living among the ruins, he collects fragments, piecing together curious connections between past and emergent mythologies and technologies.

stones *might* *fly*

These two old Cornish clinker-built punts were laid up and beyond repair. The fishermen who built them copied the streamlined shapes of the fish they caught. Now, one thousand years of wooden boat-building skills, and the fishing communities in the coves, have all but disappeared.

Commissioned by Glasgow City Art Galleries, 1991.

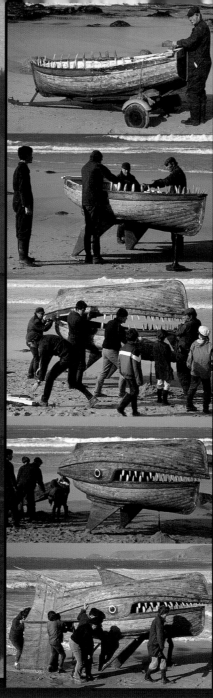

BEWARE OF THE DOG

wooden

whaler

Built from obsolete 200,000-volt heavy industrial transformer casings, and sited on a rocky outcrop, the two giant heads – an iron master and a coal miner – overlook the demolished steelworks at Consett, once the largest steelworks in Europe.

Commissioned by Sustrans North-East Long-Range Cycle Paths and Northern Arts, 1990.

DANGER
HIGH VOLTAGE

POST-
INDUSTRIAL
GIANTS

on the
Durham
Moor

The Sustrans C2C Long-Range Cycle
Path at Leadgate, County Durham.

The cycle path is on a disused railway line which carried the steel east to the shipyards of Newcastle upon Tyne.

ON WORKS—BLAST FURNA

Consett steelworks

Typographic Etching Co., Sc.

ES.

the old transformers: the legend

The men who lived here dug in the ground for the black stone.

In their giant huts, they burnt the earth and turned the sky red.

A river of steel flowed to the sea, where it was transformed into the ships, locomotives and machines that transformed the world.

13

Monday September 21st.   start laying stone.   Raining

King Coal

Workforce: local volunteers; Sustrans maintenance crew, including a stone mason, three ex-steel-workers and two ex-coal-miners.

Commissioned by Sustrans North-East Long-Range Cycle Paths and Northern Arts, 1992.

Sited on top of a slag heap in the abandoned station yard at Pelton Fell, once a colliery village on the Durham moor.

Materials: masonry from demolished railway bridge and lime kilns; 15-ton ventilation fan from a coal mine, and eight miners' shovels.

The plan: to illustrate the processes of creative thinking.

Visitors to the computer interactive Artworks Gallery climb a walkway to explore the interior of a giant brain, and create with it our six senses.

Commissioned by The Lowry Development Corporation, 1999.

creative
brian
project
for
The
Lowry

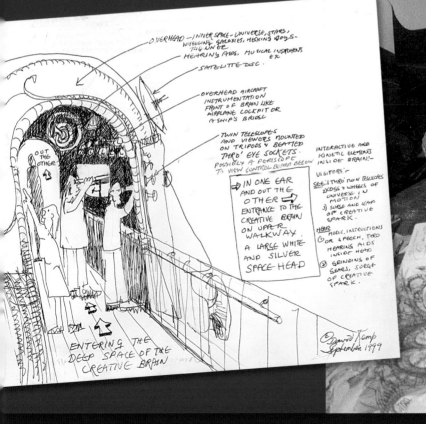

OVERHEAD — INNER SPACE — UNIVERSE, STARS, WHEELING GALAXIES, MESHING COGS— THE INNER HEARING AIDS, MUSICAL INSTRUMENTS

SATELLITE DISC. EK

OVERHEAD AIRCRAFT INSTRUMENTATION FRONT OF BRAIN LIKE AIRPLANE COCKPIT OR A SHIP'S BRIDGE

TWIN TELESCOPES AND VIEWERS MOUNTED ON TRIPODS + BEAMED THRO' EYE SOCKETS. POSSIBLY A PERISCOPE TO VIEW CONTROL PANEL BELOW

OUT THE OTHER

IN ONE EAR AND OUT THE OTHER → ENTRANCE TO THE CREATIVE BRAIN ON UPPER WALKWAY. A LARGE WHITE AND SILVER SPACE HEAD

INTERACTIVE AND KINETIC ELEMENTS INSIDE BRAIN!—

VISITORS:-
SEE: THRO' TWIN TELESCOPES CROSS + WHEELS OF UNIVERSE IN MOTION
3) SURGE AND LEAP OF CREATIVE SPARK.
HEAR
MUSIC, INSTRUCTIONS OR SPEECH, THRO' HEARING AIDS INSIDE HEAD
GRINDING OF GEARS, SURGE OF CREATIVE SPARK.

David Kemp
September 1999

ENTERING THE DEEP SPACE OF THE CREATIVE BRAIN

19

Inside
Brian's
brain.

Optic
nerves
and a
whirling
brain-
storm.

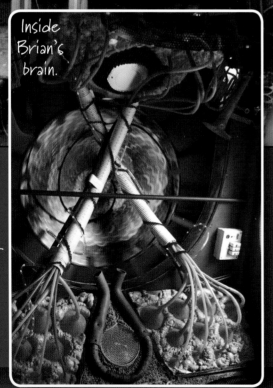

Walk
through
Brian's
head &
play with
his brain.

brian's brain

at The LOWRY

At ground-floor level,
the interactive IDEOMETER gvages new ideas.

Coiled around the ruins of an old hat factory in Manchester's culturally regenerated Northern Quarter, this unsound instrument detects the sounds of yesterday, running into tomorrow at the busy crossroads below.

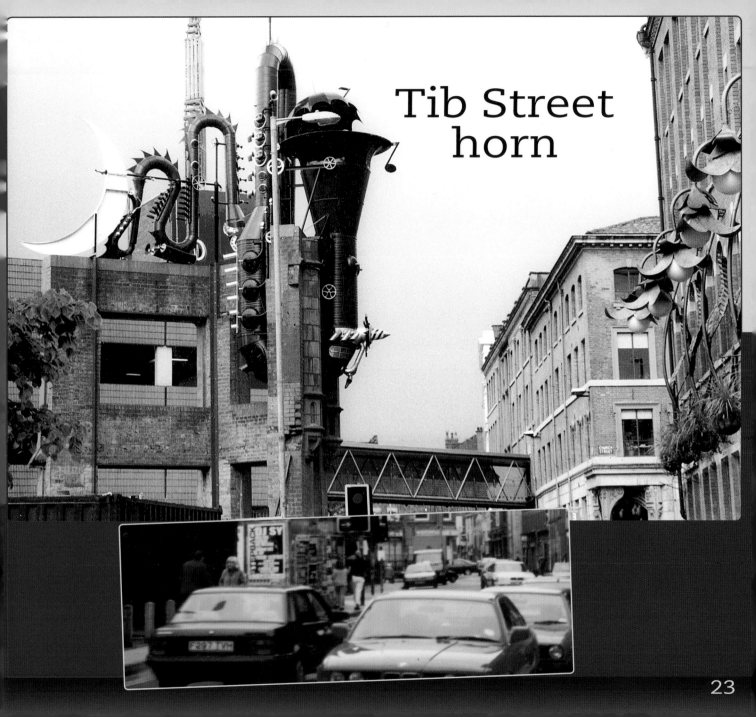

Tib Street horn

Industrialis Carbonarius Sordidus

Most varieties of the genus *Industrialis* extract energy stored in fossilized remains from ancient forests.

Industrial plants convert raw materials into an astonishing variety of useful products and harmful emissions.

Widespread overplanting causes environmental damage and climatic changes. Some scientists believe that industrial plants are burning a hole in the sky.

industrial
flame plant
at the
eden project

25

quick & easy to erect

low-maintenance

range of colours

range of formats

drought-proof

FLEXIPLANT Instant Landscapes

Synthetic FLEXIPLANTS are today's answer to modern planting schemes where instant effects are often required.

Live plants are not always sensitive to prestigious modern developments and demand constant care, attention and expensive cutting back.

FLEXIPLANTS are low maintenance, simple to install and come in a variety of formats suitable for instant on-site erections.

Available in a range of bright, modern colours in easy-clean plastic, FLEXI-PLANTS can be combined with synthetic ground cover to provide a colourful all-season solution to planting problems.

The Highway Plant range in different locations

International Manufacturing Cen

FLEXI PLANT
INSTANT LANDSCAPES

FLEXIPLANTS can be used on:
- ✓ Motorway verges and rest areas
- ✓ Decorative roundabout features
- ✓ Business parks and colleges
- ✓ Shopping malls
- ✓ Urban planting schemes
- ✓ Almost anywhere

Installation at
the Eden Project, 2000.

relics from the late iron age

Artefacts from a continuing series of 'museums from the future', reconstructing the technology, mythology, ethnology, totems and consumer cults of the late iron age.

Charioteer's helmets and other artefacts.

heavy harness

restored hare

dragonette

lost king

Dragonettes are to dragons as
maisonettes are to maisons.

future archeology

the tribe that held the sky up

There was once a clever tribe.
Their knowledge tied the four corners of the world together.
Their sorcerers had many powers.
They made great poles that held the sky up.
They had great cunning with fire.
They made the night like day.
They could send pictures in the wind.
Their long tongues could speak over many miles.
Their warriors were fierce and powerful.
They rose in the air over land and sea.
They overcame all the other tribes of the Earth.

One day, the smoke from their many clevernesses grew thick.
Great fires sprang up.
The flames licked up the poles and burnt a hole in the sky.
Slowly, the sky started to fall.
The tribe, fearing the dreadful weight of the clouds,
        dug deep holes in the earth.
Here they hide with all their clever things,
        and wait until the sky is pushed back up.

samurai

kulture vulture

unkel sam

Time stretches imponderably between past and future. Civilizations have flowered, and fallen back to Earth. Whole societies have vanished without trace. Civilizations do not usually disappear overnight. They fall into ruin and then into legend. Their artefacts become useless and are cast aside — overwhelmed by circumstance and gravity they sink into the ground, and the future rolls over them. Meanwhile, the continents continue to drift apart, the ground shudders, the Earth shakes, upheavals occur. 'Relics rising from a deep past, like bubbles in a glass of lemonade, ejected by chance and circumstance from the bowels of the Earth and collecting like froth around the rim of the rubbled ruins.' So wrote Hector Riddle Black, leader of the expedition that stumbled over a dustbin of prehistory.

ornithopter

33

fire chariot

{Trundler Sun}

Our knowledge of the last machine age is very sketchy. … The sagas of the distant 'Tekniko' and 'Mekanik' cults have been a rich source of sometimes conflicting information, but their constant and consistent references to an even earlier mythology of the omnipotent 'machines' lead us to believe that they must have some base in fact.

Recently, a major breakthrough occurred to confirm this … settlers sinking a well broke through to a long horizontal gallery.

This cavity was found to be filled with ancient artefacts, which, due to some curious element in the soil, were virtually intact and free from decomposition. While engaged in the difficult and exacting task of removing and restoring these relics (obviously an early 'Tekniko' shrine), the searchers dug deeper into the tunnel, and made an even greater find.

Behind a series of sealed walls, they discovered chamber after chamber filled with the dismantled components of a far earlier era.

The contents of most of the chambers were scattered and there seemed some evidence that items had been removed (perhaps looted by the cultists for their icons and totems).

Careful examination indicated that many of these components fitted together. Guided by the clues mythology has passed on to us, it has been possible to attempt some partial reconstruction of what must have been the sentient 'Machines' of that lost age. The main element which is missing, and of which there seems to be no trace, is the source of their motive power, the fabulous 'magic' of the White Men, their triumph and their nemesis.

telephone bill

yore mama and can-man

tailight society

released spirit

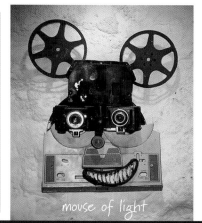
belle fellow

honkey dance mask

baglady

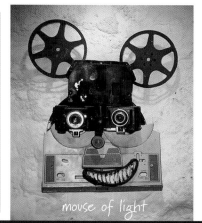
mouse of light

38

snappy tune

beast of burden

solar mask

the man who caught the sun

office dictator

masks

warm friend

men's society

main dueña

39

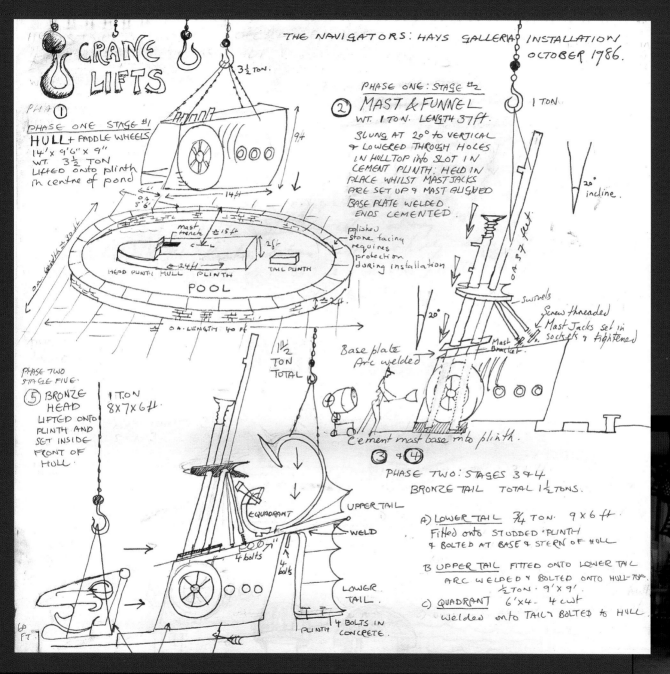

CRANE LIFTS

PHA ①

PHASE ONE STAGE #1
HULL + PADDLE WHEELS
14' x 9'6" x 9"
WT. 3½ TON
LIFTED onto plinth
in centre of pond

3½ TON.

9ft

14ft

6"
9'6"

mast trench ±15ft

2ft

24ft

HEAD PLINTH HULL PLINTH TAIL PLINTH

POOL

O.A. LENGTH 40 ft.

24"

PHASE ONE: STAGE #2
② **MAST & FUNNEL**
WT. 1 TON. LENGTH 37ft.
SLUNG AT 20° to VERTICAL
& LOWERED THROUGH HOLES
IN HULLTOP into SLOT IN
CEMENT PLINTH: HELD IN
PLACE WHILST MASTJACKS
ARE SET UP & MAST ALIGNED
BASE PLATE WELDED.
ENDS CEMENTED.

1 TON.

20° incline.

O.A. 37 feet

swivels

Screw threaded
Mast Jacks set in
sockets & tightened

Mast Bracket

polished stone facing requires protection during installation

20°

20°

Base plate
Arc welded

Cement mast base onto plinth.

③ & ④
PHASE TWO: STAGES 3&4
BRONZE TAIL TOTAL 1½ TONS.

A) **LOWER TAIL** ¾ TON. 9 x 6 ft.
FITTED onto STUDDED PLINTH
& BOLTED AT BASE & STERN OF HULL

B **UPPER TAIL** FITTED ONTO LOWER TAIL
ARC WELDED & BOLTED ONTO HULL TOP.
½ TON. 9' x 9'.

C) **QUADRANT** 6' x 4 - 4 cwt
Welded onto TAIL, BOLTED to HULL.

PHASE TWO STAGE FIVE.
⑤ **BRONZE HEAD**
LIFTED ONTO PLINTH AND SET INSIDE FRONT OF HULL.

1 TON
8 x 7 x 6 ft.

1½ TON TOTAL

QUADRANT

UPPER TAIL

WELD

LOWER TAIL.

4 bolts

4 bolts

4 BOLTS IN CONCRETE.

PLINTH

60 FT

Hay's Galleria was once a busy wharf in the Pool of London, and is now part of London Bridge City, on the Thames at Southwark.

Commissioned by St Martin's Development Corporation, 1985.

Hay's Galleria, London Bridge

The Navigators is a water feature with many moving parts. Built of bronze and steel on a myriad of found objects, the IRON FISH recalls the many vessels that docked here, and the voyages they made.

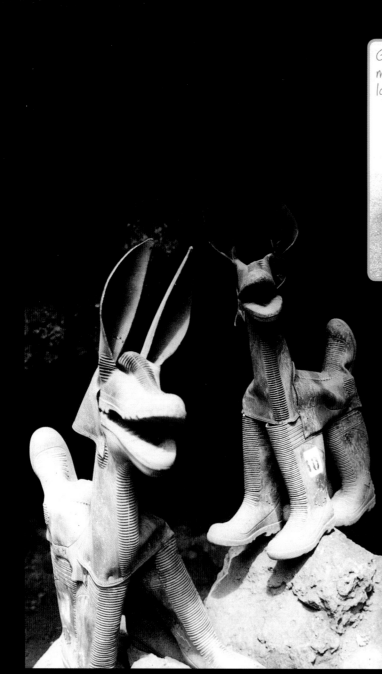

Geevor boys meet some local talent.

Geevor Tin Mine closed in 1990, ending some 2,000 years of tin-mining in west Cornwall. The workings of the 80-year-old mine reached depths of 640m, and extended one mile out under the sea.

Geevor was the victim of a massive slump in the world price of tin, which plummeted from over £10,000 per tonne in the mid 1980s to just £3,000 per tonne. Once employing 400 miners, there were only 100 left when the mine closed. Their boots were dumped.

hounds
of Geevor

Cannus Stanus Geevoriti

Relics of a vast underground workforce that rarely saw the light of day, each of these hounds fed up to three-and-a-half families. Released from their subterranean labours, they now wander the cliff-tops looking for a proper job.

bye bye

vox populaire

Mahogany, brass and steel, 10-function kinetic sculpture,
commissioned by Ogilvy & Mathers European Headquarters, Canary Wharf, London.

recent public commissions

Headquarters
Four large bronze heads for the atrium of Price Waterhouse new headquarters, Birmingham

The Hampshire Hog
Life-size bronze boar for Hampshire County Council to celebrate their centenary, outside County Hall at the Castle, Windsor

The Navigators
18-metre high steel and bronze kinetic fountain, Hay's Galleria, London Bridge.

Vox Populaire
Mahogany, brass and steel, 10-function kinetic sculpture, Ogilvy & Mathers European Headquarters, Canary Wharf, London

Chough Bowl
Bronze sculpture to commemorate the late David Penhaligon, MP for Truro.

King Coal
9-metre head in masonry and steel, Pelton Fell, County Durham

The Old Transformers
Two 6-metre high steel heads, of an iron master and a miner, at Consett, County Durham

The Lost XVII
Army in steel, unearthed at the Sustrans railway path, Kilmacolm, Glasgow

Chichester Road Gang
Group of nine figures, Sustrans railway path, Levant, Chichester

The Ancient Forester
6-metre timber and steel figure, Grizedale Forest Park, Cumbria

Heavy Plant
Large steel and masonry plant form, Sheffield Science Park

The Iron Horse
Newcastle upon Tyne Metro Station, Four Lane Ends

The Tern Project
Cast-iron bird bollards and 200-metre 'flying fence', Morecombe Promenade

Waterwheel
5-metre diameter steel and masonry wheel with fish and birds, Burrs Country Park, Bury

Tib Street Horn
Urban landmark sculpture, Northern Quarter, central Manchester

Flexiplant
Plastic plants, The Eden Project, St Austell, Cornwall

Brian's Brain
8-metre high interactive walkthrough head, aluminium and found objects, The Lowry, Manchester

Looking Both Ways
4-metre high painted steel Janus head and arch, Lloyd George Way, Cardiff

Industrial Flame Plants
6-metre high steel plants, The Eden Project, St Austell, Cornwall

exhibitions (blue indicates solo exhibitions)

1999	**Hounds of Geevor** Royal Cornwall Museum, Truro
1998–9	**Animal Magic** Edinburgh City Art Centre National Museum of Wales Touring
1998	**Weather or Not** Great Atlantic Mapworks, St Just
1997	**Art of Darkness** St Ives International Festival
1996	**Wheels of Fire (100 years of the automobile)** Wolverhampton City Art Gallery Bolton City Art Gallery
1995–6	**Serious Hot Water** Tate Gallery, St Ives
1995	**Things That Fell Apart** Ramsgate Library Gallery Centenary Exhibition, Newlyn Art Gallery
1994	**Second Sight** NCCA Durham Touring Exhibition
1994	**In a Different Light** Royal Cornwall Museum, Truro
1992	**Slaves to the Iron Horse** Rufford Country Park, Nottingham
1990	**The Tribe that Held the Sky Up** McClellan Galleries, Glasgow
1987	**Lost Leaders** The Metropole, Folkestone
1986	**Glasgow Garden Festival** Glasgow
1985	**The Tailight Society** Manchester Museum of Modern Art
1985	**The Refuse Collection** Royal Albert Museum, Exeter
1985	**Heavy Stuff** Plymouth Arts Centre

1985	Immaculate Contraptions
	Glynvivian Art Gallery, Swansea
1984	White Man's Magic
	Graves Gallery, Sheffield
	Drumcroom Gallery, Wigan
1984	Three Exhibitions about Sculpture
	Arts Council Touring Exhibition
1984	Headhunters
	Arts Council Touring Exhibition
1984	Sculpture Zoo
	Liverpool Garden Festival
1984	International Sculpture Symposium
	Yorkshire Sculpture Park
1984	A Sense of Place
	Grizedale Forest Sculpture Touring Exhibition
1983	Sculpture in a Country Park
	Welsh Sculpture Trust, Margam, Port Talbot
1982	Presences of Nature
	Carlisle Museum Touring Exhibition
1981	Fragments Against Ruin
	Arts Council Touring Exhibition
1980	Public Hanging
	Penwith Gallery, St Ives

residencies

2001	'Island of Dreams'
	Citta Vittoriosa, Malta – with Kneehigh Theatre
1999	'Ghost Nets'
	Botallack Cliffs; Tate Gallery; St Ives International – theatre & sculpture project with Kneehigh Theatre
1997	'The Women who Threw the Day Away'
	Botallack Cliffs – with Kneehigh Theatre
1996	'Ghost Nets' St Ives Bay, as above
1995	Mead Art Gallery Warwick University
1992	Sustrans Railway Paths Durham and Glasgow
1991	Bournemouth International Festival
1988	Science Park Sheffield
1987	Grizedale Forest Sculptor Grizedale, Cumbria
1985	Art Park Lewiston New York, USA
1983	Welsh Sculpture Trust
	Margam Country Park, Port Talbot, Wales
1982	Metro Sculptor, Newcastle upon Tyne
	Tyne and Wear Passenger Transport Authority

collections include

Art Park, Lewiston, NY, USA
Arts Council of England
Barbara Rockefeller
Cardiff Bay Arts Trust
Carlisle City Art Gallery and Museum
DAISI – Devon Arts Education
The Eden Project, Cornwall
Exeter City Museum and Art Gallery
The Forestry Commission
Glasgow City Art Gallery and Museum, Kelvingrove
Glasgow Museum of Modern Art
Glasgow Transport Museum
Glynvivian Art Gallery, Swansea
Hampshire County Council
John Le Carré
Liverpool Development Corporation
Lord Gowrie
Manchester City Art Gallery and Museum
MECP, Park Lane, London
National Trust, Devon and Cornwall
Northern Arts
Nottingham County Council
Pete Townsend
Price Waterhouse
Sheffield City Art Gallery and Museum
Sheffield Development Corporation
St Martin's (London Bridge) Development Corporation
Sustrans Railway Path Construction Company
Tyne and Wear Passenger Transport Authority
Welsh Sculpture Trust
Whitworth Art Gallery, Manchester
Wolverhampton City Art Gallery and Museum
Yorkshire Sculpture Park

acknowledgements

Photographs are reproduced by kind permission of: Brochocka Baynes/Lawrence Gresswell: pp. 8 (sequence), 9*; Bob Berry: pp. 2–3 (background), 37, 39 (ML); Eden Project/Bob Berry: pp. 26–7; David Gray, Sustrans: p. 11 (T); David Gray and members of the Sustrans team: pp. 16–17; Christopher Laughton: pp. 1, 2 (M), 3 (M, BL, BR), 4, 5, 42, 43; Tom Leaper: pp. 10 (R), 12 (T); The Lowry: p. 21. All other photographs are courtesy of David Kemp. The picture of Consett Iron Works Blast Furnaces on pp.12–13 is reproduced by permission of Newcastle Libraries & Information Service.

The Wooden Whaler was commissioned by Glasgow City Museums for the Art Machine exhibition organized by Triangle Projects.

First published in 2002 by **Alison Hodge**, Bosulval, Newmill, Penzance, Cornwall TR20 8XA. info@alison-hodge.co.uk www.alison-hodge.co.uk

Designed by **Christopher Laughton**.

ISBN 0 906720 60 5

A catalogue record for this book is available from the British Library.

Originated by BDP –
Book Development and Production,
Penzance, Cornwall.

Cover photograph: *Blue Bunny*.

Endpapers: *Released Spirits*.